T0065376

# Essential Counseling
# Concepts
## and
# Skills for
# Christians

**Dr. Meriann Taylor Campbell**

WESTBOW
PRESS®
A DIVISION OF THOMAS NELSON
& ZONDERVAN

WestBow Press books may be ordered through booksellers or by contacting:

WestBow Press
A Division of Thomas Nelson & Zondervan
1663 Liberty Drive
Bloomington, IN 47403
www.westbowpress.com
844-714-3454

Dr. Meriann Taylor Campbell
PO Box 321035
Flint, Michigan 48532 drmeriann@gmail.com
810-206-6336

ISBN: 978-1-6642-0993-0 (sc)
ISBN: 978-1-6642-1011-0 (hc)
ISBN: 978-1-6642-0994-7 (e)

Library of Congress Control Number: 2020921312

Print information available on the last page.

WestBow Press rev. date: 11/20/2020

# CONTENTS

Sermon: "Transformed By God" ..............................vii

Introduction ..............................................xvii

  **1.**  Personal Faith and Theology ..................... 1

  **2.**  Storytelling and Story Listening ............... 10

  **3.**  Problems in Counseling .......................... 16

  **4.**  Counseling Concepts & Terminology ...... 23

  **5.**  Counseling Skills .................................... 37

  **6.**  Scriptures for the Counselor ................... 57

  **7.**  Documentation & Information

      For Sample Counseling Forms ................. 62

Bibliography .............................................69

Endnotes ................................................ 77

About the Author ..................................... 80

# SERMON: "TRANSFORMED BY GOD"

Romans 12:2

"Don't copy the behavior and customs of this world, but let God transform you into a new person by changing the way you think. Then you will learn to know God's will for you, which is good and pleasing and perfect." (NLT)

People who seek counseling do so because they need help. They want to change something in their lives. They desire to better understand themselves and/or others. The Biblical text addresses the issue of being tempted to copy the behaviors and customs of others. Instead of yielding to this temptation, the Bible instructs us to let God transform the way we think. If we want to change, we have already done a self-assessment and made a decision to better ourselves. God desires that his way be revealed to us through his word. He desires to be made known to us. He wants us to desire his will and his ways. We are to read the Word and listen for God because the Word has the power to enlighten us, to communicate divine truth to us, and to guide us into discovering the unknown about ourselves, our world and our God. Once the Word is revealed to us, transformation can occur in us.

TRANSFORMATION means to change, to alter, to modify. God expects us to be transformed, changed, altered, and modified during our lifetime. We ought not believe the same things, or think the same way, or act the same today as we did years ago. In the text, we are told not to "copy the behaviors and customs of this world." In order to meet this mandate, we must desire change, seek after change, pray for change, and hear from the Holy Spirit. We must think before we act and abandon the belief that things just happen. Things do not just happen! They really don't. Our behavior is informed by our beliefs. Think about something you want to change. Now, think about why you haven't changed it. Do you really want to change it? Are the ways of the world enticing you, seducing you, and keeping you stuck in old behaviors?

The truth is that the ways of the world often appeal to us! We can be enticed by what we see, hear, smell, touch and feel. If we are to do as the Bible instructs and not conform to the ways of the world and not copy the behaviors and customs of the world, then we must want to do as the Bible instructs. We have to make a choice. Our will must be in accordance with God's will.

Romans 8 has much to say about the ways our flesh can control our minds. Verse 5, "Those who live according to the flesh have their minds set on what the flesh desires; but those who live in accordance with the Spirit have their minds set on what the Spirit desires." (NIV) Most of us know ourselves well enough to know what entices and seduces us, so let's take responsibility for our choices. God wants us to choose him and this is tough. It's difficult to change and if we aren't honest with ourselves, we won't change. We just won't do it! We won't even allow ourselves to know that we need to change. Remember, transformation begins in our minds. We think before we act.

Transformation can't occur without us choosing it. God won't force it on us! We often hinder our progress because we want things our way. We hold on to our list of needs, wants, and desires. We want to be strong and not be affected by the things of the world but our flesh is weak. Really weak! On a good day, we can say no and walk away. On a not so good day, we might turn and walk away. On a bad day, forget about it! We don't walk away. We cling tightly to that which feels good to us but is not good for us! Our stuff gets in the way of us doing things God's way. Our list of needs, wants, desires and urges gets in the way of us living as God instructs us to live.

In order to live righteously, we have to tell ourselves the truth about ourselves. We have to want to change. If that means avoiding certain people, places, and things, then we have to avoid certain people, places, and things! If you want to know what you believe, observe yourself. Our beliefs and actions are rarely in conflict. Our words and actions are often in conflict because we sometimes say one thing and do another. But, our beliefs and actions are rarely in conflict. What do you believe? For real. What do you believe? Be honest with yourself. Remember, your actions are informed by your beliefs!

We are responsible for our actions. Remember, things don't just happen. We make choices and then we act on those choices. We will only overcome things that separate us from God. So when our desire to please God becomes more important than our desire to do things that separate us from God! Sin separates us from God. I repeat, when our desire to please God becomes more important than our desire for sin, which separates from God, only then will we surrender to God.

The Bible tells us to be transformed by the renewing of our minds. RENEWAL means to regenerate, reconstruct, refurbish, refresh. We can only overcome sin by renewing our minds! We have to replace sinful thoughts with new, fresh, constructive thoughts. We may need to exchange negative and unhealthy people, places, and things with positive and healthy ones. It is easier said than done and it requires planning, intentionality, and prayer. It requires that we keep our eyes open and our heads clear. It requires that we take an honest look at ourselves often. It requires that we pay attention to the people we spend time with, the places we frequent, the things we do, the way we act. We must be intentional about our actions. We must keep the Word of God on our minds, in our hearts, and on our lips. We must pray often and always listen to the Holy Spirit.

While studying at Vanderbilt University Divinity School, I had the opportunity to speak privately with the late great theologian Rev. Dr. Samuel DeWitt Proctor. He asked me:

- Where do you get your information: church, TV, the Internet, your Pastor, the Bible, your friends, your family?
- Who informs your thinking?
- Who helped shape your beliefs?
- Does what you learned, as a child, still hold true for you today? The decision to ponder and answer these questions, as often as I remember them, has changed my life. The way I view others has changed because I am constantly challenged to look at myself! Those three fingers pointing back at me when I point at others, constantly convicts me to focus on Meriann!

Transformation and Renewal can happen in many ways. Such as:

- Standing on God's Word and promises.
- Reading about healing in the Bible.
- Praying about your particular need for healing.
- Listening for God in silence and meditation.

- Expecting God to hear your prayers and move on your behalf. Listening to sermons.
- Worshipping God.
- Praising God.
- Listening to praise and worship music.
- Praying more and talking less.
- Desiring and seeking after transformation, renewal, and healing. Developing a relationship with the Holy Spirit.

With the Bible as our source of information and the Holy Spirit as our Advocate (John 14:26), we can meet the mandate in Romans 12:2. With God on our side, the impossible becomes possible. We can choose to have our minds renewed and our lives transformed. Once we know the will of God for our lives, we can no longer do as we used to do and live as we used to live. We can not know what we now know! The good news is that there is another option. We need not copy the behaviors and customs of this world. We can surrender our will to God's will and God will transform us anew by changing the way we think which will change the way we act. The first step is to make the decision to surrender our will to God's will. The second step will be a glorious receipt of the promise: "Then you will learn to know God's will for you, which is good and pleasing and perfect."

AMEN

# INTRODUCTION

Theodore Walker writes in the book *Empower The People* that, "It is customary to introduce oneself, prior to engaging in conversation, because who one is makes some difference to what one says and to how what one says is understood." I believe this statement to be true; therefore, let me introduce myself. I am an African American female born in the late 1950s in the city of Flint, Michigan. As a young girl, I loved to listen to stories. Before my mom became a nurse, she was a beautician with female clients who loved to talk, tell stories, and laugh. I loved hearing the women talk and laugh. I didn't need to understand the content of their stories because I was mesmerized by their voices. I experienced the same joy, when visiting a cousin in Illinois with a beauty shop on her property. I would sweep floors and restock supplies, in order to be inside the beauty shop and listen to the women talk and laugh.

My friends and family members have often shared their cares and concerns with me. It came natural for me to listen, ask questions, and analyze situations and circumstances. I didn't have answers but I asked pertinent questions, causing my friends to feel that I helped them solve their problems. I was not surprised to learn that empathic listening was easy for me and counseling and chaplaincy appealed to me. I felt called to them and I was skilled in them.

I lived my first twenty-six years in Michigan and was educated in the public school system, Mott Community College, and the University of Michigan-Flint. At the age of sixteen, I began working as a cooperative learning student in the Traffic Department of Chevrolet Manufacturing and I worked in the automobile industry for twelve years. In the late 1980s, I relocated to Tennessee, where I lived for seven years and received my theological education from Vanderbilt University Divinity School. I loved the weather there.

The grass was green all year. In 1994, I was offered a scholarship to study psychotherapy, so I relocated to New York City. I worked in Manhattan for seventeen years, while living in Brooklyn for two years and New Jersey for fifteen years. After seventeen years in the New York metropolitan area, I returned to Michigan in 2011. At this time, I had no idea that more of my time would be spent as a patient and client than as a counselor.

I've been working on this book for several years. I decided to publish it to give back to those who've not been afforded the opportunity to study pastoral care and counseling in academia. My desire is to provide education that enhances the knowledge and skill level of those assigned to provide care and counseling to others. This publication is not meant to be all-inclusive or exhaustive.

# Chapter 1

# PERSONAL FAITH AND THEOLOGY

N THE BOOK *SAFE PLACES*, THE AUTHORS WRITE, "AS human beings, we are remarkably similar. We face the same passages in life. We are born, we grow, we age, and we die. We all have to live with other people in relationships that have difficulties. We all experience tragedies and we all suffer unpleasant consequences from willfully errant behavior or accidental mistakes. We are far more alike than we are different."[1]

In the book *The Wounded Healer*, Henri Nouwen writes, "Modern man is a suffering man psychologically wounded by lack of hope, loneliness, and rootlessness. He can only help others deal with these problems, if he is willing to go beyond his professional role and leave himself open as a fellow human being with his own wounds and sufferings."[2]

Psychotherapy is considered the talking cure. Words

and stories can help us heal. Words give voice to our experiences. Putting words into sentences and using language to express feelings can be healing. Silence can also heal. The utterances of our souls comes forth in the still quiet moments. The calmness that embraces our souls can quiet our thoughts and actions and allow us restful periods whereby transformation can occur. As a Christian counselor, I believe that God is an integral part of the counseling experience and I'm a vessel used by God to help others explore the issues in their lives that hinder them from making wise choices, living righteously, being their best self, and living their best life.

My ministry is a ministry of healing. In seeking healing and wholeness, I believe that we must take responsibility for our own lives. Only by being responsible for ourselves can we grow into our fullest potential and become all that God created us to become. Healing means living at the level of our fullest potential and liberating ourselves from anything and all things that hinder our growth and development. We know we are healed when we can experience a full range of emotions. When we take in negativity and hold onto it, it can become toxic and make us feel physically sick. Our inability to work through these negative toxic feelings and experiences often hinders our wholeness and attributes to physical and emotional illness. Some examples of such toxins include: anger, anxiety, Bible-bashing, deception, depression, disease, discomfort with our core self, drugs, envy, fear, guilt, isolation, jealousy, low self-esteem, religiosity, repression, shame, unhealthy relationships, and unhappiness.

I view my role, as a psychotherapist, as helping others identify events and experiences that have hindered their growth, development, and wholeness. As a companion on their journey to maturity, I view myself as a midwife to their therapeutic process and a co-creator to their process of growth and development. As a co-creator, I make the therapeutic environment safe, maintain clear boundaries, ask clarification questions, and express empathy. I affirm the reality that the process is painful, while monitoring the pain. Sometimes, I provide helpful hints that relieve the pain of the long and laborious process of becoming. The process of evolving can take many hours or several years. I encourage clients to stay on the journey and not abandon the process, even as their feelings, thoughts, and behaviors change. Clients can find increased safety and security in their lives, while experiencing a safe and secure therapeutic environment, where growth and healing occurs and wholeness is experienced.

In my thesis entitled *Storytelling in Family Therapy*, I wrote about my faith in God and the process of counseling. "My faith in God enables me to believe that healing and wholeness are possible. My faith in psychotherapy and the power of relationships encourages me to continue in the process of helping people create functional and healthy relationships. My faith helps me believe that psychotherapy is a medium or tool through which healing can occur. My work with clients has proven that healing happens in relationships. We often enter relationships to work out unresolved family-of-origin issues, albeit unconscious. We seek healing and wholeness in ourselves and in our relationships with others. We seek connection and union with others. If both persons are doing their work to grow, develop, relate honestly, and share intimately then the growth opportunities are endless. Some feelings and behaviors do not occur outside of a relationship because it is the relating with another person that allows past feelings and behaviors to surface. These can be wonderful opportunities to learn about ourselves. Fears of rejection and abandonment can resurface, as well as the desire to fight or flee. Having experienced such feelings in my personal life and repeatedly in therapy sessions with clients has made me a believer in the healing and transformational power of relationships."[3]

I have faith in the process of change. I believe that our laboring does indeed birth something new, wonderful, and creative. We can become new creations, new people, changed people. Something of value can come forth through the painful therapeutic process. Since I believe we are constantly evolving, becoming, and growing, I believe the process of talking and bringing unconscious materials into consciousness yields results. The process takes time. In my own psychoanalysis and psychotherapy, I learned to trust the process and have faith that something of value would come forth, eventually. Learning to 'be' versus 'do' has proven to be one of the most valuable skills I learned in my psychotherapeutic training. My ability to trust my own process of becoming enables me to trust the process of my clients. It has also caused me to realize that my clients are more than able to do their own work, which challenges my feelings of over-responsibility which are not helpful to the client's process.

Clients do not need me in their lives for them to become whole beings.

After all, they lived their lives without me, prior to entering treatment. Enabling clients to identify their coping mechanisms and affirming what works for them is imperative to their healing process. I believe that many clients know what they need to do in order to heal, albeit unconscious. Clients help teach us counselors how to help them. Their resistance to the process of counseling is oftentimes their way of teaching us that what we are doing is not working for them. Again, change is often painful. Clients with a deep desire to be whole will do so by any means necessary, even enduring the painful birthing process because of their hope for change and renewal on the other side of the pain.

# Chapter 2

# STORYTELLING AND STORY LISTENING

N *African American Pastoral Care*, Edward Wimberly defines a narrative style of communication as storytelling. Narratives draw upon personal stories and often connect personal stories to Biblical stories and the larger story of the family or culture. Storytelling and story listening have always been an integral part of Black culture and oral tradition has been the main style of communication of Black families for generations. Story listening involves empathetically hearing the story of the person involved in life struggles. Empathy means that we attend to the person with our presence, body posture, and nonverbal responses.

When I entered the psychotherapy residency training program at Blanton-Peale Graduate Institute In New York City, I knew how to listen to stories. I quickly learned that many people yearned to be seen, heard, and understood, so the experience of being the sole focus of someone's attention for forty-five minutes or more was transforming. The ability to give of myself in this way was akin to a gift to my clients, demonstrating my respect for their lives and stories. "We can only gain a better understanding of the experience of the other when we listen to their story. The words are important. The silence is important. The pauses are important. The emotions are important."[6] As we listen and attune our ears and hearts to the other, it is important to heed the following warning of Henri Nouwen: "The mystery of one man is too immense and too profound to be explained by another man."[7]

Oral tradition is a communication style that is very familiar to me.

Storytelling and story listening are definitely skills that are very much a part of psychotherapy, since we spend countless hours listening to people tell us their stories and short anecdotes. When I identify a client's communication style as that of storytelling, I find myself well equipped to listen with my third ear which means listening for the spiritual content in the story. I listen for connections between their personal story, family history, faith, and community-at-large. Using the skills of storytelling and story listening have proven helpful in building alliances with clients. They feel heard, respected, listened to, and safe to tell more stories. Even when I fail to understand their worlds, they know that I value their experiences.

The following is a fond memory of my maternal grandmother that still warms my heart today. As a psychotherapist, I have a great deal of respect for stories and storytellers. As a young girl, I remember being fascinated by the tales my maternal grandmother shared. She was a storyteller who spoke in parables and shared stories about life as a farmer in rural Arkansas. Her life had been difficult with many unpleasant twists and turns. Her stories were rarely happy ones but her face would often light up, when she spoke of the culinary delights yielded from the farm. My grandmother was a wonderful cook. I marveled at her ability to make full meals without recipes! She used a little bit of this and a small pinch of that to create delectable meals with aesthetic appeal. My aunts, mother and sisters learned the skill of cooking and creating meals like my grandmother.

I did not learn the art of cooking. I learned to listen, tell stories, and speak publicly. It began at home in the kitchen with my grandmother. As she talked, I listened while trying to make sense of her experiences, interpretations, and imagination. "Sometimes I wondered which portions of the story were real or imagined but I didn't focus too much on those details while listening to her stories." [8] I pondered these questions later, while reflecting on the information she had shared.

# Chapter 3
# PROBLEMS IN COUNSELING

NARRATIVE THERAPY USES STORIES AS metaphors to create a fuller picture of "problem-saturated stories" and the problems clients share. Problems, and the feelings associated with them, are no longer kept inside. Instead of remaining internalized, problems are externalized. The counselor helps the client externalize and focus on problems versus viewing themselves as the problem. "The person is not the problem. The problem is the problem. When counselors view clients as the problem, the client is pathologized. Externalizing the problem attempts to move the focus away from self-attack, recrimination, blame, and judgment, which are attitudes that work against productive and positive outcomes in counseling. The focus is placed on the problem's cause versus the effects or results of the problem."[9]

"My acceptance of the wisdom and abilities of my clients incorporates mutuality into the therapeutic process, as I encourage their participation in their process of evolving. While assisting clients in the process of meaning-making, I also benefit because I'm given numerous opportunities to exist and co-exist in the not-knowing and not-yet moments of therapy. Everyone involved in the counseling learns from the deconstruction and reconstruction process, as we explore the problem-free moments together. Helping clients identify 'problem-free moments' enables them to experience liberation from their problems, even if only momentarily."[10]

"The counselor is curious and persistent in gathering historical data about problems from the client and family. By interviewing several members of a family concurrently, a fuller and richer version of the problem-saturated story can be woven together."[11] The curiosity of the counselor helps at gathering the problem history and the many ways it is perceived by the individual, the family, and the community. Information gathering is so important because "prediction, certainty, and expert interpretation does not value experience of the problem. The counselor's role is to seek understanding of the client's experience so that the counselor can learn what is helpful and what is not. Problems don't occur in isolation. Problems are socially constructed. Problems are manufactured in a social, cultural, and political context."[12] When we attribute problems to the client, we can lose the cultural context of the problem and hold the individual responsible.

"When the problem is externalized, 'private thoughts are made public.' Since the problem is now externalized and the client realizes that they are not the problem, the therapist can ask questions that compare and contrast the present with the past. The client can participate in the creation of an alternative story. How is the problem affecting your life today? How did the problem affect your life yesterday. What has changed? What caused the change? How do you experience the change? These questions are solution-focused questions, helpful to separate the problem into small pieces and emphasizing positive changes, shifts, and actions."[13] Asking behavior-oriented questions can be confusing to clients. When asking solution-focused questions, clients are often able to provide more detailed information and further discuss issues.

The following is an example of focusing on the solution versus focusing on the problem:

- What brings you to counseling today?
- Has this situation happened before? What did you do then? What have you done now?
- On a scale of 1 to 10, has it worked?
- What do you want to happen?

In the book, *Solution-Focused Pastoral Counseling*, Charles Kollar wrote, "Solution-Focused Pastoral Counseling (SFPC) teaches that those being counseled have all the resources they need and God. The priority is to help the counselee get unstuck, not to generate personality change. True change occurs as a natural process of the sanctifying work of the Spirit.

The apostle Paul wrote that God is already at work

in the counselee (2 Corinthians 4:12; 1 Thessalonians 2:13). The counselee is a letter from Christ, written with the Spirit of the living God, not on a tablet of stone but on a tablet of a human heart (2 Corinthians 3:3)."[14]I believe the counselor's task is to look for this *writing of the Spirit* in the counselee's life, rather than concentrating on present or past problems.

# Chapter 4

# COUNSELING CONCEPTS & TERMINOLOGY

**M**INISTRY INVOLVES SERVING OTHERS. IN ministry, we use ourselves in our work; therefore, it is wise for us to explore our personal thoughts, biases, understandings, experiences, and feelings about others. In the ministry of pastoral care, ministers often visit their church members or persons assigned to them in hospitals and health care environments. We are rarely certain of the situation we will encounter when we visit someone. There may be things that we see, hear, and smell, that cause a reaction in us or raise a question. Nonetheless, we are NOT to speak about it in the presence of the person we are visiting! It is unprofessional and we are not visiting in order to gain knowledge about the personal details of others' lives. In addition, we never know who might be listening and we never want to hurt those to whom we are assigned to minister! Instead, we maintain our poise and pray silently about the situation and our response to it. If we find it difficult to remain in the room, we politely excuse ourselves and quietly leave the room. Later, it will be wise to speak to someone we trust about the situation and our response to it. Doing so, allows us an opportunity to learn from it.

Foundational counseling concepts and skills needed, in order to effectively minister to others, are presented in this book. When we counsel others, we develop a relationship with them. Counseling involves learning about ourselves, as we learn about others. Both the counselor and client are helped and healed through the counseling relationship. Relationship skills are needed in order to establish and maintain a healthy relationship with appropriate boundaries. The best counselors are those who have been in counseling themselves, because they have first-hand experience of what it means to be a client and participate in a counselor-client relationship. There are many people who have never been in counseling, so this book explains concepts and presents the skills needed to effectively counsel others.

The importance of hearing and listening is key because of the centrality of oral tradition in the ministry of pastoral care and counseling. Sometimes people don't know what to say, can't find words to describe their thoughts and emotions, feel overwhelmed, and more. Before utilizing scripture, prayer, anointing oil, or giving advice, listen to the sighs, moans, and groans. Listen and hear what is being said and not said. Use all of your senses. If we listen, others will tell us what we need to know. If we are willing to hear what they have to say, they will teach us how to help them. In doing so, we will better focus on the correct scripture to share and correct words to use.

## PASTORAL

The Merriam-Webster Dictionary defines pastoral as "of or relating to spiritual care or guidance especially of a congregation." We are pastoral towards others, when we are emotionally close and free of judgment and ridicule. We are pastoral, when we put ourselves aside and meet others at their point of need.

## PASTORAL CARE

Pastoral care is the art of ministering to the sick and intervening in a crisis situation using patience, comfort, all five senses, and intuition. We consciously use our senses of sight, sound, smell, taste, and touch in our work. When we think of pastoral caregivers, we often think of chaplains in hospitals, nursing homes, health care facilities and the military. In our modern era, pastoral care services extend beyond face-to-face visits to include the use of telephones, email, texting, video conferencing and more. For more information and a history of the pastoral care movement, refer to the *Dictionary of Pastoral Care & Counseling.*

"Pastoral care usually refers to all pastoral work concerned with the support and nurturance of persons and interpersonal relationships. Pastoral care includes teaching, interpreting, taking an ethical stand on the sayings of the Bible, addressing contemporary survival issues, and crisis intervention."[15]

## PASTORAL COUNSELING

"Pastoral counseling is a specialized type of care offered by the religious community to individuals, couples, families, and groups who are experiencing pain in their lives and are willing to seek pastoral help. Pastoral counseling is usually performed in hospitals, churches, and other authorized settings for ministry, by an ordained clergy person or non-ordained lay person with a commitment to a religious organization or denomination. Pastoral counselors are accountable to a religious organization, denomination, professional association. It is not a profession but a function performed by persons in the profession of ministry."[16]

"Pastoral counseling is defined as "a process of interpretation and reinterpretation of human experience within the Christian mode. Suffering in counseling is inevitable and unavoidable."[17]

"Pastoral counseling must function realistically, in order to be effective.

Ministers must consistently convey the message that

pain will not magically cease. Instead of hoping for a 'cure' in persons with whom they counsel, pastoral counselors should look for a better understanding of the issues that keep the person stuck and unable to move toward greater wholeness. When counseling is viewed as a ministry, it is a great opportunity to attend to the healing of wounds and broken relationships."[18]

"The pastoral counseling relationship is a relationship between or among persons seeking new understanding and direction for life. It is a relationship of hope and expectation that the Holy Spirit will accompany the counselor and counselee as they experience God's mediating power.

The pastoral counselor places his or her trust in the workings of the Holy Spirit. Final outcomes are left to a larger process than that of the counseling experience alone."[19] In my experience, the hope of the counseling experience is that the counselor will be able to enter the counselee's world, so that both may grow.

## THE PASTORAL COUNSELOR

According to Charles Gerkin, "pastoral counselors approach the Bible differently than Bible scholars and theologians. Searching for images, themes, symbolic figures, analogies, and stories that prove helpful, pastoral counselors realize that they bring an awareness of the mystery of the ultimate and incarnate to all counseling situations and events. They draw upon their worldview, religious tradition, interpretation of the Bible, and personal experience."[20]

"Pastoral counselors listen to counselees and assist them in interpreting their stories. When persons seek a pastoral counselor, they are seeking someone who will listen to them, especially in times of crisis. Pastoral counseling is a process of dialogue and interpretation that can involve more than the counselor and counselee. It can extend to include family members, extended family members, and friends. The communication may be verbal and nonverbal, especially in moments of grief and despair. Sometimes, a pastoral presence is all that is required to provide comfort to persons in distress. Songs, poems, words of encouragement, home visitations, telephone calls, and prayer can also be helpful."[21]

## HEALING

"Healing is the process of being restored to bodily wholeness, emotional well-being, mental functioning, spiritual aliveness, religious salvation, and broken human relationships. Healing is also the development of a just social and political order among races and nations."[22]

"Healing is God's work. There is no healing without God. Through prayer we can come into intimate contact with God, the source of all healing, bringing our lives into line with God's healing activity. Prayer helps to discern God's healing and wholeness, so that we can cooperate with these activities."[23]

# GUIDING

"Guiding is advising, counseling, teaching, mentoring, directing, leading, showing, piloting, and steering. Guiding is goal-setting, sharing resource information, role-modeling, and providing constructive criticism and feedback. The counselor directs the counselee to pray for direction from God, as both agree to address specific issues and concerns."[24]

# SUSTAINING

"Sustaining is to prop up, carry, support, endure, feed, maintain, nourish, provide comfort. Sustaining entails acknowledging that persons are in distress and experiencing a catastrophic event." [25]

"Sustaining is to comfort, strengthen, stand alongside, and lend support and encouragement when a situation cannot be immediately changed.

Sustaining is to carry on a ministry of sustenance, as long as circumstances preclude healing, i.e., crisis counseling."[26]

## RECONCILING

"To reconcile is to reunite, restore harmony, adjust, settle, alleviate, relieve. Reconciliation is future-oriented. Once issues have been identified and goals have been set, part of the healing process is problem-resolution and doing what needs to be done in order to avoid stagnation. Part of reconciliation is seeking forgiveness of oneself and others, once there is acknowledgement of harm to oneself or others."[27]

## TRANSFERENCE: HOW WE AFFECT OTHERS

Transference is the psychological term for how we affect others. Whenever we are in contact with others, there is a reaction. When something about us reminds a client of someone else, they react. Sometimes the reaction is rational. At other times, the reaction is irrational. It is normal to experience an internal or external reaction to others. However, the client is responsible for his/her actions and the way that they express themselves!

Our awareness of transference can arm us with information that allows us to respond appropriately to others and assist them in responding appropriately to us. Ask the client, "Do I remind you of anyone?" If the answer is yes, ask about his/her relationship with this person. How do you feel in my presence? Do you feel like you can do counseling with me? If not, a referral is necessary. If you need help processing the experience, it is wise to consult with a mental health professional.

## COUNTERTRANSFERENCE: HOW OTHERS AFFECT US

Countertransference is the psychological term for how others affect us. Whenever we are in contact with others, there is a reaction. Clients can trigger memories, thoughts, and feelings in us. When something about them reminds us of someone, we react. Sometimes the reaction is rational. At other times, the reaction is irrational. It is normal to experience an internal or external reaction to others. However, we are responsible for our actions and reactions!

Our awareness of countertransference can arm us with information that allows us to respond appropriately to others. Ask yourself, "Who does this client remind me of? What was my relationship with them? Can I work with this client?" If your answers are yes, then proceed with the counseling. If your answers are no, refer the client to another counselor. Consult with a mental health professional, in order to process your experience.

# Chapter 5
# COUNSELING SKILLS

## PASTORAL PRESENCE/IDENTITY

A S A REMINDER, THE WORD PASTORAL MEANS of or relating to spiritual care or guidance especially of a congregation. We are pastoral towards others when we are emotionally close and free of judgment and ridicule. We are pastoral when we put ourselves aside and meet others at their point of need. Pastoral presence is sometimes called pastoral identity. Our identities, as pastoral persons, affect every area of our lives because of the way that we experience the world and are experienced in the world. How we feel about ourselves is reflected in the way we present ourselves to others (i.e., our facial expressions, style of dress, posture, tone of voice, energy, emotional stability, etc.)

We often think about pastoral presence in relation

to hospital chaplains and clergy persons who wear religious symbols and attire (i.e., crosses, robes, stoles, etc.) Our physical and spiritual energy reveal our level of emotional and social well-being (i.e., lethargic, happy, depressed, sad, positive, calm, chaotic, negative, pessimistic, optimistic, etc.)

## SELF-CARE

Each person who comes for counseling is seeking something. It takes great courage to realize that one needs help and then seeks help. Honor the person's process and presence. Prepare yourself. Expect your life to be impacted through your work in the ministries of visitation and counseling. The people we meet can bless us, as well as grieve us. It is not possible to avoid being affected by others but we can avoid feeling overly stressed and overwhelmed. Working with people is stressful. Once we understand and accept this, we can better attend to our specific needs. How do you react to stress? Do you drink alcoholic beverages, overeat, act out destructively, use street drugs, manage prescription drugs unhealthily, become hostile or manic? Do your own personal assessment regularly. A healthy food plan is not an option! Attend to your dietary needs daily and pay special attention to the timing of your cravings and destructive acting out.

Self-care is extremely important just as much as our physical, and mental health is important. Self-care is our responsibility. It's very important that we regularly engage in activities that relieve stress, before we feel sick or

get overwhelmed. Explore activities that interest you and help you manage stress and anxiety. A few suggestions include: reading, writing, walking, running, talking, singing, laughing, sleeping, praying, dancing, massages, therapy, cleaning, drawing, painting, cooking, baking, meditating, exercising, etc. Utilize community resources in your area. If you need help, find a counselor or join a therapeutic group. If you need more counseling education, find a class. If you feel a need to debrief often, find a trained mental health professional to assist you in the debriefing process.

## EFFECTIVE LISTENING & HEARING SKILLS

When we listen, we use more than our ears. We use all of our senses. We are present physically, emotionally and spiritually. Before the client enters the counseling room, we clear the clutter from our minds so as to be totally available to them. We prepare ourselves and focus on where we sit, how we sit, our facial expressions and body posture. We do not speak much. Listening can appear easy but effective listening is a skill that must be learned and practiced.

We listen differently depending on the person, place, situation, crisis, number of people involved, etc. We do not interrupt or help people finish their sentences. Sometimes, we listen quietly without responding, trusting that our listening is enough. At other times, we listen actively with minimal responses. It is important to know that others are rarely trying to entertain us when they share their stories with us. They are trying to tell us something about themselves and our job is to hear what they are saying, as well as what they are NOT saying. Nonverbal communication is very informative and just as meaningful as verbal communication. Try not to become too involved in the details or drama of the story, so as not to lose your perspective or ability to pay attention to the person telling their story. It is important to understand the motivation and meaning behind the story, as this gives you more information about the storyteller.

Edward Wimberly, in the book *African American Pastoral Care*, defines story listening as hearing the story with empathy. When we can listen with our whole self, the listener feels seen, heard, cared for, attended to, and understood. Listening with our whole self includes our eyes, ears, sense of smell, taste, touch, and intuition. Our body language says that we are present and attentive. Since hearing and speaking simultaneously is not effective, we talk very little. We ask questions and avoid making assumptions.

Developing effective hearing and listening skills is of utmost importance in the ministries of counseling and visitation. Before utilizing scripture, prayer, anointing with oil, or giving advice, we must listen to those with whom we counsel and visit. If we are willing to listen, they will often tell us what we need to know about them and their situation. If we are willing to hear what they have to say, they will often teach us how to most effectively and efficiently meet their needs.

## CONFIDENTIALITY

Counselors are taught to "Do No Harm" to their clients, purposefully or mistakenly. Clients are to be treated with respect at all times and their information should be kept private. We should not discuss what we see or hear with others, neither those in our homes or our churches. It is sometimes difficult to refrain from telling others about our encounters, but we must avoid discussing details with family and friends. When people share their life stories with us, they are sharing a part of themselves and their stories warrant confidentiality. Handle the information of others with care.

Sometimes, we cannot stop thinking about something we have seen or heard. We need to talk about it. When this happens, debrief with a trained professional or minister who also does counseling and visitations. The person's name and identifying information can be changed, in order to maintain confidentiality. Focus on YOUR thoughts, feelings, and discomfort. Avoid the temptation to judge or gossip.

All forms that contain identifying client information should be kept secure. When staff members are off-site, the files should be locked. When clients are on the premises, staff should know their whereabouts at all times. Keys should be kept separate from the file cabinet. Staff members should refrain from talking about clients inside and outside of the office, within listening distance of persons not directly involved in the organization.

Avoid discussing the details of a client's history with family and friends. Information should be handled with care, just as the person sharing the information should be handled with care. We should only share the stories of our clients in peer supervision, clinical supervision, teaching situations, employee group meetings or during the referral process. The names and other identifying information of clients should be changed in supervision and teaching situations. We honor the information that clients share with us by avoiding the temptation to judge, gossip, or preach about them and their personal lives.

## SACRED SPACE

In preparing for a counseling session, I give myself time to set up the room. "As sacred space, the counseling room becomes a space in which to sit in the presence of a child of God who is entrusting me with their life story, a story deserving of honor and witness. God is in the midst of the counseling relationship, as the counseling relationship develops between the counselor, client and God. As a spiritual midwife, I become an enlightened witness to the story of the client and my challenge becomes that of consciously and consistently viewing the client as a child of God who is being molded by God."[28]

## APPOINTMENTS

When making appointments, it is important to plan your visit with the person. Which days of the week, times of the day, and locations are convenient and inconvenient for you? It is better to avoid making an appointment, then to make an appointment and be unable to keep it. It is difficult to accept that we cannot save the world or meet the demands of all people! We are not Jesus, so we must let go of our savior complex. Do what you can. Be realistic.

## VULNERABILITY

Do not expect clients to walk through the door and share their personal details immediately. We may be a stranger to them and people rarely immediately trust strangers; therefore, clients must grow to trust us. Trust does not happen immediately. Trust must be earned. First impressions are important. When people share too much information too fast, they usually feel vulnerable and act defensively. Once trust is earned, strive to continue to be worthy of the client's trust. Listen to what your clients have to say and respect their vulnerability and privacy. Realize that it is very difficult to:

(1) admit a need for help,

(2) ask for help, and

(3) accept help.

When counseling others, use a private space with a door, whenever possible. If a private space is not possible, position your body to allow for optimal privacy. For example, if others can see into the room or you are not in a space with doors, make sure the client's back is facing others. Do your best to protect the client's identity. It is okay for others to see your face. Protect the client from being identified.

## THE INITIAL CONTACT

Expect the Holy Spirit to be present in your sessions. Let yourself know that you are not the healer. You are a human vessel through which healing occurs. God is the healer. Pray for the client. Pray for yourself. Before you meet with someone in need, focus on quieting your thoughts. Center yourself. Pray for the presence and aid of the Holy Spirit. Prepare to avoid the urge to judge what you hear, see, smell, think, or feel and keep your negative thoughts, opinions, and assumptions to yourself. Many people are in crisis when they come to us for help or we visit them. Their situation has placed them in a position where we are present to offer comfort, emotional support, and spiritual nurture. Be aware of how you present yourself. The attention should not be on you, so your attire and demeanor should not call for attention. Do not wear loud smelling cologne or perfume, as many people are sensitive to smells.

The intake process begins the moment contact is made with the client. First impressions are important. When gathering information from clients, do so in a non-threatening manner. When the interview is done in person, use a private space. When a private space is not available, position your body and the client's body to allow for optimal intimacy. For example, have the client face you with their back to others. Make it a goal to leave a good impression on every client every time you have contact with them.

## ASSESSMENTS

When clients come to Pastoral Counselors, their expectations are different than when they go to other mental health professionals. They expect the advice and assistance to be more holistic and spiritual. They expect kindness, comfort, and help to better manage their lives and control their circumstances. Often, they come for help when they are in the midst of a crisis and without a support system. The counselor then becomes an integral part of their support network.

Since the assessment process entails the gathering of information, the intake person must listen more than she or he talks. Use your senses to help you learn what is really going on with the client. Ask questions. Do not assume that you know or understand what is happening. Document your findings as soon as possible after each interview. Try not to make assumptions. Ask specific questions and seek additional details when you do not understand something that a client has said or done. Try to be as objective as possible when writing what you see and hear.

As you gather information from the client or their representative, evaluate the client's level of functioning. Is she or he emotionally stable enough to engage in this interview process? Is she/he reality-oriented and able to tell you; Who they are? Where are they? What year is it? Why are they in your office? If the client cannot answer these basic questions, it is highly unlikely that a thorough interview can occur at this time. A counselor should be prepared to handle emergency situations, as we sometimes see a client who is mentally incapacitated, unstable, highly agitated, etc.

## COUNSELING RESISTANT CLIENTS

When someone asks for help but does not seem to want it, they are resisting change. A resistant client consciously wants our help but is seldom willing to change their behavior. Resistant clients are often hostile and silent. They often give confusing messages, conflicting information, laugh inappropriately, talk constantly, intellectualize situations, make a scene, and act out for attention. They may keep their appointments and talk about their problems with you but do not easily accept the help that is offered and available. These are unconscious defenses against changing their behavior. Expect excuses about why your suggestions won't work!

Resistant clients can be very difficult and frustrating to us. Resistant clients can easily induce anger in others. It is important that we pay attention to our reactions, so that we do not become angry. We must remain patient and focused. Avoid being seduced into their drama and hysterics. Pay attention to your body language and monitor your tone of voice. Listen and observe their behavior. Give them permission to receive or deny the help you've offered. Avoid taking responsibility for trying to heal them and do not force them to accept the help you offer. Consult with a mental health professional for help processing your experience, as resistant clients can trigger a host of emotions.

## COUNSELING RELUCTANT CLIENTS

When someone refuses to ask for help, go for help, or accept help, they are reluctant to change. In order to avoid changing, they may delay asking for help or ignore their problems. When they are sent to others for help, they might keep the appointment but refuse to talk or give erroneous information, talk in circles, or give confusing and conflicting information. Sometimes reluctant clients clearly express their anger at the person who sent them for help. They may even project their anger onto you, the counselor.

Reluctant clients have usually been given an ultimatum which means they have been identified as the person with the problem. When they walk into our offices, they are often being punished by someone. They only come to see us because we are their last resort for help! As a helper, our role is to listen. Do not talk much. Do not argue and avoid taking responsibility for the client or their situation. They may blame you and/or others for what is happening to them but avoid blaming yourself or trying to force them to cooperate with you. Allow them to share their feelings about being forced to seek help. Give them time to accept you and the help you are offering. Be patient. Keep your focus and realize that you cannot heal them, force them to change, or make them accept the help you offer. Consult with a mental health professional for help processing your experience, as reluctant clients can trigger a host of emotions.

## REFERRALS

There are times when a Pastoral Counselor needs to refer a client to another counselor. Have a conversation with the client about the referral. The client should have a clear understanding regarding the reason for the referral. It is not always possible to get the client to agree with the need for the referral but the reason for the referral should be clearly delineated and discussed, as well as the type of service they can expect to receive, and contact information for the new counselor.

Research your community and surrounding geographical area for other Pastoral Counselors and mental health professionals. Get written permission from your client, before sharing their history with another counselor. Remember, the client's information is confidential. The written permission allows you to share their information. Make sure that both the client and new counselor have accurate information in writing. Place a copy of the referral in the client's chart. There should be a closure session, when possible. During the final session, offer the client the opportunity to share their experiences. It is important to bring closure to your time together.

"The counselor and the counselee must be in agreement with God's *intention* if the counselee is to make any progress. The Apostle Paul encourages the Christian to press forward toward God's unfolding purpose, trusting God each step of the way. In the same passage he also instructs us to 'live up to' what we have already attained." (Philippians 3:12-15, NIV) This *assumes that God has already placed into our lives much of what He considers necessary for us to begin making progress regarding our spiritual and emotional growth.*" [29]

# Chapter 6

# SCRIPTURES FOR THE COUNSELOR

*Romans 15:13, "May the God of hope fill you with all joy and peace as you trust in him, so that you may overflow with hope by the power of the Holy Spirit." (NIV)*

- Pray for ourselves, as vessels used by God in our counseling sessions.
- Pray for the presence of the Holy Spirit in our counseling sessions.
- Pray for focus during our counseling sessions.
- Pray for our clients.
- Give God praise for all things.

*Psalms 71:5, "For thou art my hope, O Lord GOD: thou art my trust from my youth." (KJV)*

- Do not take anything for granted.
- Be grateful for our life.

- Be grateful for the lives of our clients and their loved ones.

- Identify, acknowledge, and work on and through negativity in our life.

- Have faith that God will meet our needs.

- Have faith that God will meet the needs of our clients.

*Hebrews 4:16, "Let us therefore come boldly unto the throne of grace, that we may obtain mercy, and find grace to help in time of need." (KJV)*

- Read the Bible.

- Set and maintain healthy and permeable boundaries with our clients.

- Acknowledge our fears.

- Create plans to better manage and eventually overcome our fears.

*Matthew 7:7-8, "Ask and it will be given to you; seek and you will find; knock and the door will be opened to you. For everyone who asks receives; the one who seeks finds; and to the one who knocks, the door will be opened." (NIV)*

- Acknowledge the potential for dual relationships with our clients, as we may see them in the community and at local churches.
- Maintain a practice of reading and studying the Bible.

*Psalms 71:3, "Be thou my strong habitation, whereunto I may continually resort: thou hast given commandment to save me; for thou art my rock and my fortress." (KJV)*

- Avoid the temptation to fulfill our social needs through our clients.
- Develop and maintain a strong prayer life.

*Psalms 103:1-5, "Bless the LORD, O my soul: and all that is within me, bless his holy name. Bless the LORD, O my soul, and forget not all his benefits: Who forgiveth all thine iniquities; who healeth all thy diseases; Who redeemeth thy life from destruction; who crowneth thee with lovingkindness and tender mercies; Who satisfieth thy mouth with good things; so that thy youth is renewed like the eagle's." (KJV)*

# Chapter 7

# DOCUMENTATION & INFORMATION FOR SAMPLE COUNSELING FORMS

## DOCUMENTATION

WHETHER YOU WORK ALONE, WITH A TEAM of counselors, or in an agency, it is important to keep records on each client. Whenever there is contact with a client, a description of the contact should be documented. We don't want to rely on our memory, as it is possible that we will not accurately remember the details.

While working on records that contain client information, be aware of the location of clients in the work environment. Records should be kept in a confidential location, as they contain identifying information. It is important to keep the records in a locked container or file cabinet. If you work alone, it is still important to keep the records in a container or file cabinet. If you work in an office, make sure the file cabinet is locked before you leave the office. We don't want to inadvertently share confidential client information or handle the information casually. Remember, it is the responsibility of the counselor to maintain client confidentiality at all times.

There may be reticence to documenting our contacts with others. We don't want the information to be used against us and we don't want others to know that we have records on them.

## INFORMATION FOR SAMPLE COUNSELING FORMS

RECORD OF CLIENT CONTACT

Name of Client(s)

Day, Date, Time

Notes

Signature of Counselor

CLIENT ASSESSMENT FORM

Day, Date, Time, Fee $

Name(s)

Home Phone

Cell Phone

Who Referred You?

Relationship Status: Married, Single, Separated, Living
Together, Divorced

Who Lives with You?

Why Are You Seeking Counseling?

Physical Health Issues

Mental Health Issues

Alcohol & Drug History

Goal 1

What will you do to reach this goal?

Goal 2

What will you do to reach this goal?

Goal 3

What will you do to reach this goal?

Signature of Counselor

Date

Signature(s) of Client(s)

Date

SUPERVISION DOCUMENTATION FORM

Day, Date, Time

Client's Name(s)

Name of Counselor

Concern #1:

Suggestions:

Concern #2:

Suggestions:

Concern #3:

Suggestions:

Supervisor's Comments

Additional Notes

Counselor's Signature

Date

# RELEASE OF CLIENT INFORMATION FORM

Day, Date, Time

I/We, _____ agree to the release of my/our counseling records to the counselor or organization listed below:

Name of Counselor

Name of Organization

Street Address

City, State, Zip Code

Signature(s) of Client(s) & Date

Signature of Counselor & Date

# BIBLIOGRAPHY

Arterburn, S., F. Minirth, and P. Meier. <u>Safe Places:</u> <u>Finding Security in the Passages of Your Life</u>. Nashville, TN: Thomas Nelson Publishers, 1997.

Baruth, Leroy G., and M. Lee Manning. <u>Multicultural</u> <u>Counseling and Psychotherapy: A Lifespan Perspective</u>. Englewood Cliffs, NJ: Prentice-Hall, Inc., 1991.

Bates, Kathy. <u>Broken Spirit to Boundless Joy: How to</u> <u>Break Through Your Hurts and Take Back Your Life</u>. Rochester, NY: Psalm 23 Ministries, 2019.

Bowen, M. <u>Family Therapy in Clinical Practice</u>. New York, NY: Jason Aronson, 1978.

Brezena, Ben. <u>Living In Jesus: Growing In The Life We Were Made To Live</u>. Newnan, GA: Christian Families Today, 2019.

Clinebell, Howard John. <u>Basic Types of Pastoral Care & Counseling: Resources for the Ministry of Healing & Growth</u>. Revised and Enlarged. Nashville, TN: Abingdon Press, 1984.

Clinebell, Howard John. <u>Counseling for Spiritually Empowered Wholeness: A Hope-Centered Approach</u>. New York: Haworth Pastoral Press, 1995.

Clinton, Tim and Ron Hawkins. <u>The Quick-Reference Guide to Biblical Counseling</u>. Grand Rapids, MI: Baker Books, 2009.

Collins, Gary R. <u>Christian Counseling: A Comprehensive Guide</u>, 3<sup>rd</sup> Edition. Nashville, TN: Thomas Nelson, Inc., 2006.

<u>Dictionary of Pastoral Care and Counseling</u>. Rodney J. Hunter, General Editor. Nashville, TN: Abingdon Press, 1990.

Fielder, Cain Hope. Troubling Biblical Waters: Race, Class, and Family. Maryknoll, New York: Orbis Books, 1989.

Frantz, T. T. Death And Grief In The Family. The Family Therapy Collections. Rockville, MD: Aspen Systems Corporation, 1984.

Gerkin, Charles V. Widening the Horizons: Pastoral Responses to a Fragmented Society. Philadelphia, PA: Westminster Press, 1986.

Hendrix, H. Getting The Love You Want: A Guide For Couples. New York, NY: Harper & Row Publishers, Inc., 1988.

Hendrix, H. Keeping The Love You Find: A Personal Guide. New York, NY: Pocket Books, 1992.

Johnson, W. Brad. The Minister's Guide to Psychological Disorders and Treatment. United Kingdom: Routledge, 2014.

Joseph, Courtney. Ecclesiastes: Wisdom for Loving Well: An In-depth Bible Study. Charlotte, NC: Women Living Well Ministries, 2016.

Kennedy, Eugene and Sara C. Charles. On Becoming A Counselor: A Basic Guide for Nonprofessional Counselors. New Expanded Edition. New York, NY: Crossroad Publishing Co., 1996.

Kollar, Charles Allen. Solution-Focused Pastoral Counseling: An Effective Approach for Getting People Back on Track. Grand Rapids, Michigan: Zondervan, 1997.

Lucado, Max. God Will Use This for Good: Surviving the Mess of Your Life. Nashville, TN: Thomas Nelson, Inc., 2013.

Martin, Catherine. The Calling: The Story of Who You Are and Why You Are Here. Palm Desert, CA: Quiet Time Ministries Press, 2019.

McGoldrick, Monica, John K. Pearce, and Joe Giordano. Ethnicity and Family Therapy. New York, NY: The Guilford Press, 1982.

Miller, Alice. The Body Never Lies: The Lingering Effects of Cruel Parenting. New York, NY: Norton, 2005.

Miller, Alice. The Truth Will Set You Free: Overcoming Emotional Blindness & Finding Your True Adult Self. New York, NY: Basic Books, 2001.

Minuchin, S. Families & Family Therapy. Cambridge, MA: Harvard University Press, 1974.

Monk, Gerald, John Winslade, Kathie Crocket, and David Epston. Narrative Therapy in Practice: The Archaeology of Hope. California: Jossey-Bass, 1997.

Moore, Thomas. Care Of The Soul: A Guide For Cultivating Depth And Sacredness In Everyday Life. New York, NY: HarperCollins Publishers, 1992.

Muller, Wayne. <u>How, Then, Shall We Live? Four Simple</u> <u>Questions That Reveal The Beauty And Meaning of</u> <u>Our Lives</u>. New York, NY: Bantam Books, 1996.

Nouwen, Henri J. M. <u>The Wounded Healer: Ministry</u> <u>in Contemporary Society</u>, 1ˢᵗ ed. New York: Doubleday, 1972. Simon, Sidney B., and Suzanne Simon. <u>Forgiveness:</u> <u>How To Make Peace With Your Past And Get On With</u> <u>Your Life</u>. New York, NY: Warner Books, Inc., 1990.

Switzer, David K. <u>The Minister As Crisis Counselor</u>. Revised and Enlarged. Nashville, TN: Abingdon Press, 1974.

Taylor, Meriann. <u>Models Of Care-Giving In Black</u> <u>Baptist Churches</u>. Nashville, TN: Vanderbilt University Divinity School, 1992. Master of Divinity Senior Project.

Taylor, Meriann. <u>Storytelling In Family Therapy</u>. New York, NY: Blanton-Peale Graduate Institute, 1998. Marriage & Family Therapy Residency Program, Certificate Project.

Taylor, Meriann. The Wounded Healer As An Enlightened Witness In The Pastoral Counseling Relationship. New York, NY: New York Theological Seminary, 2011. Doctor of Ministry Demonstration Project.

Underland-Rostow, Vicki. Shame: Spiritual Suicide. Shore wood, MN: Waterford Publications, 1995.

Whitfield, Charles. Healed the Child Within. California: Health Communications, 1987.

Wimberly, Edward P. Prayer in Pastoral Counseling: Suffering, Healing and Discernment. Louisville, KY: Westminster/John Knox Press, 1990.

WomanistCare: How To Tend The Souls Of Women. Linda H. Hollies, editor. Joliet, IL: Woman To Woman Ministries, Inc. Publications, 1991.

# ENDNOTES

1   Arterburn, Minirth, and Meier, "Safe Places: Finding Security in the Passages of Your Life," xi-xii.

2   Nouwen, Henri, "The Wounded Healer: Ministry In Contemporary Society," front book flap.

3   Taylor, "Storytelling In Family Therapy," 42, 48.

4   Ibid., 50.

5   Ibid., 50-51.

6   Taylor, "The Wounded Healer," 55.

7   Nouwen, 63.

8   Taylor, "The Wounded Healer," 54.

9   Monk, Winslade, Crocket, and Epston, "Narrative Therapy In Practice: The Archaeology of Hope," 6, 26.

10  Taylor, "Storytelling In Family Therapy," 42.

11  Monk et al., 7.

12  Ibid., 27.

13  Taylor, "Storytelling In Family Therapy," 7.

14 Kollar, Charles Allen, "Solution-Focused Pastoral Counseling: An Effective Approach for Getting People Back on Track," 16, 38.

15 "Dictionary of Pastoral Care and Counseling," 832-833, 845.

16 Ibid., 845, 849-850.

17 Ibid., 157.

18 Taylor, "Models Of Care-Giving In Black Churches," 13.

19 Charles Gerkin, "Widening the Horizons," 100-101.

20 Ibid., 15.

21 Ibid., 14.

22 Ibid., 499.

23 Edward P. Wimberly, "Prayer in Pastoral Counseling," p. 11.

24 Taylor, "Models Of Care-Giving In Black Churches," p. 26.

25 Ibid., 26.

26 "Dictionary of Pastoral Care and Counseling," p. 193-194.

27 Taylor, "Models Of Care-Giving In Black Churches," p. 28.

28 Taylor, "The Wounded Healer", vi.

29 Kollar, p. 19.

# ABOUT THE AUTHOR

Dr. Meriann Taylor Campbell is a Pastoral Psychotherapist who specializes in treating individuals, couples, and families dealing with issues of trauma, women's health issues, chronic illness and pain, grief and loss, incest and rape. She focuses on solutions and resilience versus problems. Dr. Campbell worships at Kingdom of Heaven Ministries in Flint, Michigan where Dr. Lonnie Brown and Frances Brown are co-founders. She was ordained in 1992 by Rev. Edwin Sanders and the Metropolitan Interdenominational Church in Nashville, Tennessee.

Dr. Meriann received her Associate of Applied Science Degree from Mott Community College, Bachelor of Applied Science degree from the University of Michigan-Flint, and Masters of Divinity degree in Pastoral Care & Counseling from Vanderbilt University Divinity School.

She also received a Certificate in Marriage & Family Therapy from Blanton-Peale Graduate Institute in New York City and a Doctorate of Divinity degree in Pastoral Psychotherapy from New York Theological Seminary.

Clinical credentials: Michigan Limited Marriage & Family Therapy License, Diplomate and Board Certified Expert in Traumatic Stress from the American Academy of Experts in Traumatic Stress.

Dr. Meriann lives in Michigan with her husband Kevin Lennell Campbell, Sr. She finds great joy in spending time with her husband, family, friends, and Emotional Support Animal Keno, a mixed-breed beagle dog. Meriann's hobbies include: listening to praise and worship music, singing, reading, and writing. In her quiet time she enjoys meditation, prayer, Bible reading, and playing mahjong and solitaire.

Printed in the United States
By Bookmasters